# The Gifts of the Spirit

# THE GIFTS OF THE SPIRIT

by

W. T. Purkiser

Beacon Hill Press of Kansas City
Kansas City, Missouri

Copyright, 1975
Beacon Hill Press of Kansas City

ISBN: 0-8341-0347-8

Printed in the United States of America

# Contents

# Preface

This small book is an expansion of a chapter in the author's volume *God's Spirit in Today's World*. It is offered in this form because of the widespread interest in a more intensive treatment of the gifts of the Spirit in Christian life and service.

While major attention is given to the gifts, it would be a serious error to consider the gifts without relating them to the fruit of the Spirit. This we shall attempt in a closing chapter. No Christian need choose, for the Holy Spirit gives both gifts and graces. Yet while a Christian without the exercise of his gifts is largely useless, a Christian without the fruit of the Spirit would be a contradiction of terms. "I am the true vine," said Jesus, "and my Father is the gardener. He cuts off every branch in me that bears no fruit, while every branch that does bear fruit he trims clean so that it will be even more fruitful" (John 15:1-2).

There is always danger in considering gifts that we neglect the Giver. When we seek God for himself and not just for His gifts, we are likely to have both. If we seek only His gifts, there is a good chance we shall find neither the Giver nor the gifts. Thomas a Kempis said, "A wise lover considereth not so much the gift of his lover as he doth the love of the giver. He regardeth more the love than the gift."[1]

For this reason we first take a look at "The Giver as Gift." In the presence and fullness of the Holy Spirit there is that qualification for life and service He has for each of us.

—W. T. PURKISER

# ¶

# The Giver as Gift

The Holy Spirit is himself both Gift and Giver. He must be known to us as Gift before He can be known as Giver.

## I. THE SPIRIT IN CONVERSION

Everything God does for us in salvation we have through the immediate agency of the Holy Spirit. Daniel Steele described him as "the Executive of the Godhead." Just as all the functions of government reach and affect the individual citizens through its executive branch, so all that comes to us from God in Christ reaches us through the Spirit.[1]

### 1. The Holy Spirit Convicts of Sin

There is a natural conscience in the human heart that protests when one does what he deems to be wrong. Many of our earliest ideas of right and wrong come from parents and teachers. But in and through all moral intuitions, there is "the true light that gives light to every man" (John 1:9) brought to us in prevenient grace by the Spirit of Christ. He is the "cosmic Conscience," the unrecognized Source of all human morality—Christ "anonymously present" in moral consciousness.

While a guilty conscience may lead one to seek relief in religion, a genuine awakening to the need of Christ is the work of the Holy Spirit. He convicts of sin, righteousness, and judgment, as Jesus said He would (John 16:8-11). The sinfulness of sin shows up in the light of His purity. The winsomeness of righteousness appears in the light of His love. The certainty of judgment confronts us in the light of His holiness.

## 2. The Holy Spirit Draws Us to Christ

"The Spirit . . . [says], 'Come!'" (Rev. 22:17). Without that invitation we would neither want to nor be able to come. The drawing pull of the Father without which no person can come to the Saviour is the tug of the Holy Spirit (John 6:44).

## 3. Conversion Is Being "Born of the Spirit"

What theologians call "regeneration" literally means "being born again" or "born anew." Jesus said to Nicodemus, a very religious member of the Jewish Sanhedrin, "I tell you the truth, unless a man is born of water and the Spirit, he cannot enter the kingdom of God. Flesh gives birth to flesh, but the Spirit gives birth to spirit. You should not be surprised at my saying, 'You must be born again.' The wind blows wherever it pleases. You may hear its sound, but you cannot tell where it comes from or where it is going. So it is with everyone born of the Spirit" (John 3:5-8).

Paul echoes the truth in slightly different terms: "He saved us, not because of righteous things we had done, but because of his mercy. He saved us through the washing of rebirth and renewal by the Holy Spirit, whom he poured out on us generously through Jesus Christ our Savior, so that, having been justified by his grace, we might become heirs having the hope of eternal life" (Titus 3:5-7).

10

### 4. *The Spirit Witnesses to Our New Life*

Christian assurance is not the result of wishful thinking nor is it the conclusion of logic alone. "Those who are led by the Spirit of God are sons of God. For you did not receive a spirit that makes you a slave again to fear, but you received the Spirit who makes you sons. And by him we cry, '*Abba*, Father.' The Spirit himself testifies with our spirit that we are God's children. Now if we are children, then we are heirs—heirs of God and co-heirs with Christ, if indeed we share in his sufferings in order that we may also share in his glory" (Rom. 8:14-17).

The witness of the Spirit is not an emotion, although it may result in deep peace and great joy. It is the deep and settled conviction—coming with greater force than any intuition—that what God has promised He has done. It is the assurance with which we call God our Father and know that His grace has justified us and made us His children.

It is clear, then, that we do not first meet the Holy Spirit in a second crisis or baptism. Everyone who is a Christian in the New Testament sense has been brought to the Saviour and made a new creation in Christ by the active agency of the Holy Spirit. Paul could say with complete certainty: "And if anyone does not have the Spirit of Christ, he does not belong to Christ" (Rom. 8:9).

## II. THE SPIRIT AS THE GIFT OF CHRIST AND THE FATHER

Not only does the Bible teach that all saving grace is mediated by the Holy Spirit; it also indicates that there is a "gift of the Spirit" or a fullness or baptism with the Spirit that is given only to those who are already part of the Church as a community of believers. Unless New Testament terminology is carefully observed, there is apt to be confusion at this point.

It is sometimes difficult for people to distinguish between the impartation of the Holy Spirit in regeneration and receiving the Spirit as Christ's gift to His Church. But the distinction is essential to an understanding of the order of salvation. One must "have" the Spirit before the Spirit really has all of him. One must be born of the Spirit before he can be baptized or filled with the Spirit. It is only to those regenerated by the Spirit that He becomes the sanctifying Lord (2 Cor. 3:17-18).

Jesus' first promise of the Holy Spirit concerned His coming as the Gift of a Father to His children: "If you then, though you are evil [*poneros*, a word that means not only morally evil but subject to labor, pain, and sorrow], know how to give good gifts to your children, how much more will your Father in heaven *give* the Holy Spirit to those who ask him!" (Luke 11:13, italics added).

The promise is more explicit in John 14:15-17, "If you love me, you will do what I command. I will ask the Father, and he will give you another Counselor, the Spirit of truth, to be with you forever. The world cannot accept [receive] this Counselor, because it neither sees him nor knows him. But you know him, for he lives with you and will be in you."

The Father's Gift of the Spirit is sent by the ascended Lord, so that as the divine Gift—in theological language—He "proceeds from the Father and from the Son" (John 15:26; 16:7).

It is quite true that these promises have an immediate reference to the first Christian Pentecost in Jerusalem as recorded in Acts 2. But there is every evidence that they are experiential as well as historical. When Jesus did pray, as He said He would, He said, "My prayer is not for them alone. I pray also for those who will believe in me through their

12

message" (John 17:20), a qualification that takes in every Christian from the apostolic age to the present.

The promise of John 14:15-17 is quite explicit. It is a promise made to those who love Christ and keep His commandments. While the world is the object of the Spirit's convicting and regenerating work, "the world cannot receive" (KJV, RSV, etc.) Him. Only those who "see him" and "know him" are in a position to "receive him."

Further, Jesus said to those to whom the Spirit was to be "given," He is *with* you and will be *in* you." That the "with" and "in" are not to be taken spatially in the sense of "outside of" and "inside of" is seen in the preceding verse, where the Spirit's presence is described as being "with you forever"; and in verse 23 when, in the fulfillment of the promise, Jesus said, "If anyone loves me, he will obey my teaching. My Father will love him, and we will come to him and make our home *with* him" (italics added).

The essential point is not therefore that One who has been hovering outside will now come in. Nor is it a matter, as has sometimes been claimed, of having "part" of the Holy Spirit first and "all" of Him later. As a Person, the Holy Spirit is indivisible and all He does for us is done "inside."

The essential point is rather *what* the indwelling Spirit does for us: regenerating in His first work and sanctifying wholly in His infilling as the divine Gift in the second work (1 Thess. 5:23-24). The regenerating Spirit becomes our sanctifying Lord. Those who were "born of the Spirit" are "baptized with" or "filled with" the Spirit.

Jesus further says that "the gift my Father promised" is that baptism with the Spirit of which John had spoken. "Do not leave Jerusalem, but wait for the gift my Father promised, which you have heard me speak about. For John baptized with water, but in a few days you will be baptized with the Holy Spirit" (Acts 1:4-5).

When the promised Spirit came, He did not fill the

13

3,000 who were converted at that first Christian Pentecost. He convicted them through the witness of Peter and the others. He baptized or filled only those who were qualified according to the terms Jesus had earlier set forth: who loved Him and kept His commandments, who were not of the world, with whom the Spirit was present, and who knew Him in His regenerating power.

When the multitudes asked anxiously, "'Brothers, what shall we do?' Peter replied: 'Repent and be baptized, every one of you, in the name of Jesus Christ so that your sins may be forgiven. And you will receive the gift of the Holy Spirit'" (Acts 2:37-38).

Those who have argued that repentance and the forgiveness of sins are identical with receiving the gift of the Holy Spirit have failed to notice the importance of water baptism here. Though the interval need not be long, and probably was not, the fact that repentance and the forgiveness of sins were to be publicly acknowledged by water baptism as a condition for receiving the gift of the Holy Spirit shows the necessary time sequence in the order of salvation. James Moffatt clearly expresses the force of the original in his translation of verse 38: "'Repent,' said Peter, 'let each of you be baptized in the name of Jesus Christ for the remission of your sins; then you will receive the gift of the holy Spirit.'"

While there are minor ambiguities in some cases, every instance of persons being filled with the Holy Spirit in the Book of Acts reveals prior conversion or spiritual life.

It was Christians in prayer who were filled with the Holy Spirit in Acts 4:31.

The Samaritans believed and were baptized (Acts 8:12). They later "received the Holy Spirit" (Acts 8:14-17).

Saul of Tarsus was already "Brother Saul" when Ananias visited him, waiting obediently in prayer (Acts 9:11, 17). The purpose of the visit was that Saul's sight might be

14

restored and that he should "be filled with the Holy Spirit" (Acts 9:17).

Cornelius, "devout and God-fearing," prayerful, heard in heaven (Acts 10:1-4), knowing the gospel (Acts 10:37), was not a typical unregenerate man. The Holy Spirit came upon him and others of his family as Peter preached (Acts 10:45)—an event Peter himself equated with Pentecost (Acts 11:15-16; 15:8-9).[2]

The 12 at Ephesus were "disciples," the name typically applied to Christian believers in the Book of Acts (19:1; cf. 11:26). Paul accepted their faith without question (19:2) and baptized them in the name of Christ, a clear testimony to their prior faith (19:5). After this, "the Holy Spirit came on them" and, like the original band of disciples in Jerusalem 25 years before and those with Cornelius 15 years earlier, they spoke other languages—a sign that the gospel had again broken beyond its original Palestinian limits.

Use of the same English word "gift" for the Spirit himself and for what He imparts to His people can easily cause confusion for us. Readers of the New Testament in its original language would have had no difficulty at this point. The word used in speaking of the Spirit himself as the Gift is *dorean*—a term that means in Greek rather precisely what *gift* means in English. On the other hand, as we shall see more at length in the next chapter, the term used for the many gifts the Giver imparts to individual Christians in the Church is *charismata*.

We see then that the Giver is himself the Gift of the Father and the Son to His people. At any level of Christian experience, the spiritual gifts are given. But it is to those who permit Him to abide fully as their sanctifying Lord that the Holy Spirit of God gives His gifts most freely.

# 2

# What Are Spiritual Gifts?

Nothing is more important in practical Christian service than the recognition and use of the gifts of the Spirit. While Christians throughout the centuries have had and used spiritual gifts, it has only been in recent years that the Church has given much attention to this aspect of the ministry of the Holy Spirit.

As with other doctrinal themes, we have been made more aware of the importance of spiritual gifts by the very confusion and misunderstanding that has grown up around them. Extreme claims have been made for some of the gifts, and outright fanaticism has developed. Yet there is a body of biblical teaching that should be studied and taught. Darkness is never driven from a room with a club but by letting in the light.

## I. The Meaning of Charismata

The New Testament has a special word for spiritual gifts. It is *charismata*, from which we get the current English adjective *charismatic*. *Charis* is the New Testament Greek word for "grace." It was used in classical Greek to mean "beauty, charm, attractiveness," and, by easy extension, "favor, kindness," and "gratitude" as felt on the part of the receiver.

When New Testament writers took over the term

*charis*, they used it to describe the spontaneous, beautiful, unearned love of God at work in Christ Jesus. *Charis*, "grace," as A. M. Hunter says, "means primarily the free, forgiving love of God in Christ to sinners and then the operation of that love in the lives of Christians."[1]

Stemming from *charis*, *charisma* is a singular noun that literally means "grace gift." It stands for any of the spiritual endowments Christians have in varying degree and form. This is of course a far cry from the popular use of *charisma* to describe the glamor, winsomeness, or personal magnetism of some popular political figure or star of stage or screen.

*Charismata* is the plural form of *charisma* and means "gifts of grace." The *charismata* are defined as "divinely conferred endowments." *Charismatic* describes men or movements emphasizing or manifesting the gifts of God through His Spirit.

*Charisma* and *charismata* occur 17 times in the New Testament—16 times in the writings of the Apostle Paul and once in 1 Pet. 4:10-11. The range of grace-gifts is extremely broad. A total of 20 abilities or bestowments are identified. It is rather clearly implied that even this is not intended to be a complete catalogue of all the ways the Holy Spirit empowers His people.

## II. Kinds of Gifts

Paul's listings of the gifts of the Spirit may be broadly grouped into "General Gifts" and "Service Gifts."

### 1. General Gifts

In the New Testament use of the term, all Christians are charismatic. There are two *charismata* conferred on all who receive Christ as their personal Saviour.

*a.* The first such *charisma* is *justification.* Paul wrote in Rom. 5:15-16, "The gift *[charisma]* is not like the trespass. For if the many died by the trespass of the one man, how much more did God's grace and the gift that came by the grace of the one man, Jesus Christ, overflow to the many! Again, the gift of God is not like the result of one man's sin: The judgment followed one sin and brought condemnation, but the gift *[charisma]* followed many trespasses and brought justification." What a precious spiritual gift God has given us all in forgiveness of sins and reconciliation with himself!

*b.* The second universal Christian spiritual gift is *eternal life.* Rom. 6:23 says, "For the wages of sin is death; but the gift *[charisma]* of God is eternal life through Jesus Christ our Lord" (KJV).

These two are the indispensable gifts. If one does not have the gifts of justification and eternal life, he may be a Christian in name, but he is none of Christ's in point of fact (Rom. 8:9). But Paul speaks of four other general *charismata.*

*c.* The apostle's own ministry, first by personal presence and now by the written word, is a spiritual gift: "I long to see you so that I may impart to you some spiritual gift *[charisma]* to make you strong" (Rom. 1:11).

*d.* The manifestations of God's mercy to His people are *charismata.* It is in this context that Paul wrote, "God's gifts *[charismata]* and his call are irrevocable" (Rom. 11:29).

*e.* A particular station or condition of life is cited as one of the *charismata* in 1 Cor. 7:7—"I wish that all men were as I am. But each man has his own gift *[charisma]* from God."

*f.* Answered prayer is a *charisma* indispensable to the work of God (2 Cor. 1:11).

18

## 2. Service Gifts

The "service gifts" are the most typical examples of what we usually describe as spiritual gifts. It is with these that most interest has developed in recent years and with which we shall be concerned through the remainder of this book.

## III. SERVICE GIFTS AND TALENTS

The service gifts of the Spirit are the abilities and powers given to the people of God for their usefulness in Christian service. H. Orton Wiley defined spiritual gifts as "the divinely ordained means and powers with which Christ endows His Church in order to enable it to properly perform its task on earth."[2]

"The gifts of the Spirit, then," Dr. Wiley writes, "are supernatural endowments for service, and are determined by the character of the ministry to be fulfilled. Without the proper functioning of these gifts, it is impossible for the Church to succeed in her spiritual mission. Hence the subject is of great importance, not only to theology, but to Christian experience and work."[3]

A special committee studying the work of the Holy Spirit for one large denomination reported that "charismata may be defined as endowments and capacities necessary for the edification and service of the Church, bestowed by the Holy Spirit upon its members, in virtue of which they are enabled to employ their natural faculties in the service of the Church, or are endowed with new abilities and powers for this purpose."[4]

The gifts of the Spirit are to be distinguished from natural talents or "gifts" inherent in an individual's temperament or personality, although there is a close relationship between them. Spiritual gifts often function through natural faculties. But spiritual gifts extend beyond the pure-

19

ly natural as the Holy Spirit channels His life-giving power through the endowments He bestows.

While spiritual gifts are imparted by the Holy Spirit, our use of them is subject to development. Rarely does a gift emerge full-blown. Spiritual gifts, like natural talents, must be discovered and cultivated. In Rom. 12:6-8, Paul indicates that gifts are to be consciously used "in proportion to . . . faith," "generously," "diligently," and "cheerfully." As natural talents are sharpened and improved through training and practice, so spiritual gifts are made more effective as we develop them through faithful use.

True spiritual gifts differ from talents in that natural talents and abilities may be developed and used solely for personal satisfaction. They can be quite egocentric. The gifts of the Spirit, on the other hand, are all related to what has aptly been called the "body life" of the Church.[5] They are the individual Christian's contribution to the life of the Christian community of which he is a part.

This does not mean that one's spiritual gifts are not a source of deep satisfaction to the individual. Although primarily outgoing in relation to the Church's body life, the proper stewardship of spiritual gifts has a reflex effect upon the individual. The Christian who uses his gifts is not only a blessing; he is blessed himself.

Just as the use of natural talents is one of the sources of highest satisfaction, so the discovery and use of spiritual gifts is a source of deep and abounding joy. To be used by God and consciously to cooperate with the Holy Spirit in developing the gifts He gives brings the greatest sense of fulfillment possible to the Christian heart.

## IV. All Christians Have Gifts

In addition to the general *charismata* of justification and eternal life (Rom. 5:15-16; 6:23), every Christian has at least one service gift. Both Paul and Peter make this point. It is of the individual members of the Church that Paul says, "We have different gifts, according to the grace given us" (Rom. 12:6). "To each man the manifestation of the Spirit is given for the common good" (1 Cor. 12:7). "Each one should use whatever spiritual gift he has received to serve others, faithfully administering God's grace in its various forms" (1 Pet. 4:10).

Wherever Christians are idle in the work of the Church as the body of Christ, it is because they have failed to discover and use their spiritual gifts. There is no Christian without at least one service gift. It is part of being a Christian in the New Testament sense.

The other side of the picture is that, wherever important work in the local church is not being done, the reason is not that no one can do it but that some are failing to use the gifts God has given them. The Church at large today is afflicted with a serious unemployment problem: not of people looking for work, but of work looking for people. Wherever this condition is found, both the church and its individual members are impoverished and growth is stunted.

One clear implication of Rom. 12:3-8 and 1 Cor. 12:12-26 (where gifts are placed in the context of the body life) is that in every local congregation there are people with gifts to accomplish all that congregation ought to be doing in the kingdom of God. Every true function of the body of Christ has a "member" to perform it, and every member has a function to perform.

One great problem of the Church everywhere is the number of those whose spiritual gifts are dormant, unrecognized, or unused. Gifts, like talents, may be buried for years —to come to light when new demands come. It is important to discover and develop these spiritual gifts, just as it is important to discover and develop natural talents. The Church will never be complete or adequate until increasing numbers of members take an active part in its ongoing work through the use of their unique and irreplaceable gifts.

How do we recognize our spiritual gifts? Usually in the same way we recognize natural talents—by the satisfaction that comes from trying. The person with a talent for singing will find enjoyment in singing. One who is naturally talented in leadership will find fulfillment in leadership.

Spiritual gifts—like the talents to which they are related —are many times recognized by others before we see them ourselves. Many times one is called to a Kingdom task either by a divine inner impression or by invitation of leadership before his gifts are fully known and developed. The needed gifts appear as the responsibilities are shouldered.

Gifts are given for use, not admiration or personal ego-building. The Spirit's gifts and God-assigned responsibilities go together.

To ignore the gifts of the Spirit is to slight the Giver— something no sincere Christian would wish to do. For the sake of the Church primarily, but for our own satisfaction in Christian service, it is important that we find and use the gifts the Spirit has given us.


## V. Principles of Distribution

In 1 Corinthians 12, Paul gives three principles that govern the distribution of special service gifts of the Spirit:

1. All spiritual gifts are given for profit or value. The measure of the worth of any gift is the degree to which it serves the interests of the whole Church (1 Cor. 12:7; 14:6, 19). While special value to the individual has been claimed for some of the gifts of the Spirit, such is not the emphasis of the New Testament. *All* spiritual gifts are for one purpose —to build the body. In this sense, all are equal. "Now to each man the manifestation of the Spirit is given for the common good" (1 Cor. 12:7).

All gifts have value in that they contribute to the body life, but not all are of equal value. We are directed to "eagerly desire the greater gifts" (1 Cor. 12:31). Speaking to men "for their strengthening, encouragement and comfort" is vastly superior to speaking in an unfamiliar language (1 Cor. 14:1-3). No gift, however great, can compare with the overriding value of love, without which all gifts are valueless (1 Cor. 12:31—14:1).

2. Different gifts are given to different persons according to the sovereign will of the Spirit (Rom. 12:6; 1 Cor. 12:11-18, 28-30). The gifts given are related to the responsibilities resting with each Christian. While each Christian has at least one gift, all do not have the same gift nor should any expect to have them all. Because of this, no gift—however genuine or spectacular—can be made an evidence of the baptism with the Spirit or even of spirituality in any degree. Immature and even carnal Christians may excel in gifts (1 Cor. 1:7; 3:1-3; etc.).

This point is particularly stressed in 1 Cor. 12:29-30. Here, the form of the questions in the original Greek New Testament demands a "No" answer in each case: "Are all apostles? Are all prophets? Are all teachers? Do all work miracles? Do all have gifts of healing? Do all speak in tongues? Do all interpret?" The best English translation of these questions would be something as follows:

"All are not apostles, are they?
"All are not prophets, are they?
"All are not teachers, are they?
"All do not work miracles, do they?
"All do not have gifts of healing, do they?
"All do not speak in tongues, do they?
"All do not interpret, do they?"
The only possible answer is "No."

3. The variety of spiritual gifts is for the purpose of unifying, not dividing, the Church (1 Cor. 12:14-27). Per-

sons with differing gifts need others to round out the life of the whole. Paul's striking comparison of the Church as the body of Christ drives home the truth with unmistakable force. The gifts are many; the Spirit is one. The members of the body have varied functions; the body is an organic whole. "If the whole body were an eye, where would the sense of hearing be? If the whole body were an ear, where would the sense of smell be? But in fact God has arranged the parts in the body, every one of them, just as he wanted them to be. If they were all one part, where would the body be? As it is, there are many parts, but one body.

"The eye cannot say to the hand, 'I don't need you!' And the head cannot say to the feet, 'I don't need you!' On the contrary, those parts of the body that seem to be weaker are indispensable, and the parts that we think are less honorable we treat with special honor. And the parts that are unpresentable are treated with special modesty, while our presentable parts need no special treatment. But God has combined the members of the body and has given greater honor to the parts that lacked it, so that there should be no division in the body, but that its parts should have equal concern for each other" (1 Cor. 12:17-25).

Whatever Paul's words may mean concerning the modesty with which the "unpresentable parts" are to be treated, the analogy certainly warns against what we would call exhibitionism in relation to any gift of the Spirit.

# The Romans List

The Apostle Paul gives two lists of special or service gifts of the Spirit. The first is in Rom. 12:6-8: "We have different gifts [*charismata*], according to the grace given us. If a man's gift is prophesying, let him use it in proportion to his faith. If it is serving, let him serve; if it is teaching, let him teach; if it is encouraging, let him encourage; if it is contributing to the needs of others, let him give generously; if it is leadership, let him govern diligently; if it is showing mercy, let him do it cheerfully."

There are seven gifts listed here:

## 1. Prophesying

"Prophesying," or "prophecy" as in the KJV, is repeated also in the Corinthians list. It is one of the gifts that is apt to be most confusing to us. To the modern ear, "prophesying" suggests predicting, foretelling the future. It could, of course, include this.

But in the New Testament, prophesying means much more than predicting. Paul defines it in 1 Cor. 14:3 as speaking "to men for their strengthening, encouragement and comfort." More than foretelling, prophecy is forthtelling the Word of God to those who need to hear. The Greek term is *propheteia*, from *pro*, "forth," and *phemi*, "speak." It was widely used in the first-century world to describe one who proclaims a message or interprets the oracles of the gods—and when Christians used it, of the one true God.

While the gift of prophesying is most naturally the characteristic gift of those who preach the gospel, it is important to note that it is the one gift Paul recommends most highly for all Christians: "Follow the way of love and eagerly desire spiritual gifts, especially the gift of prophecy" (1 Cor. 14:1). The entire fourteenth chapter of 1 Corinthians is given to a contrast between the gift of prophecy and the practice of speaking in unfamiliar languages. Speaking "to men for their strengthening, encouragement and comfort" is the highest possible use of language.

Peter gives "speaking the very words of God" as a spiritual gift (1 Pet. 4:10-11). In terms of the use of words today, it stands for Spirit-anointed preaching, teaching, and witnessing. In such speaking, the words of a human being become the word of God, bringing conviction and light to those who hear. Thousands of men and women in the Church in every age use the gift of prophecy with telling effect.

Such speaking is to be for each "in proportion to his faith" (Rom. 12:6). Like the sowing of seed, speaking the Word of God is an act of faith. It is with faith that the truth will "accomplish that which" God pleases and "prosper in the thing whereto" He sends it (Isa. 55:11, KJV).

There is a secondary sense in which "faith" here may mean the individual's understanding of the content of the gospel. The Greek is literally "the faith" *(tes pisteos).* We speak, teach, and witness best in proportion to our grasp of the truth. God's part is to anoint; ours is to provide Him something to anoint by study, meditation, and prayer.

## 2. Serving

"Serving" is the second gift in the Romans list. *Service* here is *diakonia* in the Greek New Testament. The KJV translates it "ministry." It is the word from which *deacon* and *deaconess* come. It usually refers to ministering to the physical needs of people, as for example in Acts 6:1-2, where it is translated "daily ministration" in the KJV and where it involved the serving of tables.

Peter also mentions the gift of serving. "If anyone serves, he should do it with the strength God provides, so that in all things God may be praised through Jesus Christ" (1 Pet. 4:11).

One who serves from the basis of a gift of the Spirit may do very much what others would do from humanitarian motives. There will be two differences, however. The spiritual gift results in heightened effectiveness through the infused power of the Spirit. And the motive will clearly be what Peter indicated—"That in all things God may be praised through Jesus Christ."

A visitor to a mission to lepers watched a missionary nurse tenderly cleanse and dress the ugly sores of her patients.

"I wouldn't do that for a million dollars," he said.

"Neither would I," was the missionary's reply. "I wouldn't do it for a million dollars; I do it for the love of Christ."

Such is the gift of serving. It must be used: "Let him serve." Most Christians come under condemnation, not for what they do, but for what they do not do. The word of doom at the judgment is, "Inasmuch as ye did it not . . ." (Matt. 25:45, KJV). Stephen Winward writes, "It does not follow that our lives are blameless because we have done nothing wrong. Having done nothing may itself be our sin. Our gravest sins often are omissions—the word of encouragement left unspoken, the opportunity missed, the work neglected, the duty shirked, the helpful deed undone."[1]

There is special blessing in the gift of serving. Jesus himself said, "I am among you as one who serves" (Luke

22:27); and, "Whosoever will be chief among you, let him be your servant: even as the Son of man came not to be ministered unto, but to minister, and to give his life a ransom for many" (Matt. 20:27-28, KJV).

In the kingdom of God, service is not a stepping-stone to stardom. It is itself the highest nobility, because one who serves becomes most like the Master. Toyohiko Kagawa put it incisively:

> I read
> In a book
> That a man called
> Christ
> Went about doing good.
> It is very disconcerting
> To me
> That I am so easily satisfied
> With just
> Going about.[2]

### 3. Teaching

The third gift on the Romans list is teaching—*didaskon* in the Greek. This is instructing and grounding others in the truth. Other gifts—such as "the word of wisdom" and "the word of knowledge" (KJV) from the Corinthians list—are closely related to and involved in teaching.

Teaching is of supreme importance in the work of the Church, second only to prophecy or preaching. While preaching and teaching overlap, the general distinction is that preaching is appealing to action while teaching is providing instruction. New Testament scholars often distinguish between *kerygma*, the proclamation of the gospel to the world, and *didache*, the instruction of those already converted.

Teaching is the function of the pulpit, the church

school, and the Christian home. It is expounding in detail what is proclaimed in preaching. It includes powers of understanding, explanation, analogy, and application which must be given by the Holy Spirit if spiritual fruit is to be the outcome.

Teaching is not only by word but includes example and the subtle influence of character. Arthur Guiterman said it well in his familiar lines:

> *No printed word nor spoken plea*
> *Can teach young hearts what men should be,*
> *Not all the books on all the shelves,*
> *But what the teachers are, themselves.*

One Sunday school teacher, a graduate nurse by profession, wrote a "Teacher's Pledge." She adapted it from the famous "Oath of Hippocrates" administered to medical doctors upon graduation and from the "Florence Nightingale Pledge" for nurses. It is worthy of note by all who would develop the gift of teaching:

> I solemnly pledge myself before God and in the presence of this assembly to pass my life in purity and to practice Christianity faithfully. I will abstain from whatever is harmful and mischievous and will do all I can to transform myself and those I teach into genuine children of God. I will do all in my power to maintain and elevate the standards of teaching Christ and will hold as precious each soul committed to my keeping, and will share all inspiration and experience that comes to my knowledge in the practice of my calling. With loyalty will I endeavor to aid the minister and leaders in their work and devote myself to the upbuilding of the kingdom of God.

While teaching is named as a *charisma* of the Spirit, it is only fair to note that the human skills and knowledge involved are subject to training and development. "If a man's gift is . . . teaching, let him teach," the apostle writes. That is, "let him [*really*] teach"—equipping himself so far as he can with all it takes to teach effectively.

A true teacher is the lead learner in the group. Jesus said, "Therefore every teacher of the law who has been instructed about the kingdom of heaven is like the owner of a house who brings out of his storeroom new treasures as well as old" (Matt. 13:52). To bring out "new treasures as well as old" means continually putting something new into the storeroom of understanding and memory. Failing to do this means that soon all that will come out is old.

In this respect, Christian teaching is like preaching. Its effectiveness depends on the energy of the Spirit channelled through it. The Holy Spirit does actually bring to mind truths that need to be imparted. But the Holy Spirit works through memory. "The Counselor, the Holy Spirit, whom the Father will send in my name, will teach you all things and will remind you of everything I have said to you" (John 14:26). What Jesus said is now available to us through the Gospels. But the Spirit cannot "remind" us of what Christ said unless we have learned it from His Word.

## 4. Encouraging

Exhortation or encouragement is the next service gift the apostle lists. The Greek term is *paraklesis,* the same root from which *Paraclete* or "Comforter" is derived. It literally means "going to another person's help" in whatever way he may need that help. Phillips translates it here as "stimulating of the faith."

Encouragement or comfort is the application of this gift to the past, "putting heart into" those who have suffered defeat or loss or who are going through trials. *Parakaleo*, the verb form from which *encouragement* comes, literally means "to call alongside"—to be with another to help him.

Encouragement may be conveyed by just the presence of another as well as by the spoken word. Times of sorrow and bereavement call for the exercise of this gift by other members of the fellowship. One who practices encouragement ministers "grace in the wilderness" (a phrase from Jer. 31:2, KJV) to others in their "wilderness" of loneliness, suffering, bereavement, or doubt. In a world such as this, the gift of encouragement or comfort will always be needed in large supply.

Exhortation, on the other hand, is the application of this gift to the future, challenging others to pursue some course of action. The action needed may be a commitment to Christ in either repentance or consecration—hence the use of the term in the sense of exhorting. It may be an appeal to service, to ideals of conduct, to carefulness in Christian living.

True Christian preaching, in the sense that we understand it today, always involves this gift in good measure. The preacher of today, like the Old Testament prophet, has the double responsibility of "comforting the afflicted, and afflicting the comfortable." As we saw in relation to teaching, preaching is distinguished from instruction by the essential appeal to action which is involved. The gift of exhortation aids others in lifting their horizons, deepening their commitments, and purifying their purposes.

## 5. Contributing to the Needs of Others

"Contributing to the needs of others"—giving or sharing—is the next *charisma* the apostle lists. This means more than giving from a philanthropic spirit. It means giving from a heart filled with God's kind of love. In giving, we become most like the Master, who "gave himself" for His Church (Eph. 5:25); and the Father, who "gave his one and only Son" (John 3:16).

The last three gifts on Paul's Romans list each contain a word of direction. Giving is to be done "generously";

those with the gift of leadership are to "govern diligently"; showing mercy is to be practiced "cheerfully." Giving can be niggardly and grudging. When it is a spiritual gift, it is to be generous.

This gift is more than the practice of Christian steward-ship. Stewardship requires no special spiritual gift. It is part of Christian discipleship and common to all true followers of the Lord Jesus, however they may differ in definition and detail.

The gift of giving includes the ability to earn and give money for the advancement of God's work with such wisdom and cheerfulness that the recipients are strengthened and blessed. Giving can be irresponsible and actually harmful. Giving as a *charisma* of the Spirit is strengthening and permanently helpful.

Just as teaching involves mastering subject matter to be taught, giving involves abilities to earn and get that which may be given. God has blessed certain people with almost a "Midas touch." It seems that everything they touch turns to gold. A number of these have also had the gift of giving, both motivation and insight to invest their material wealth in Kingdom causes.

Few in the history of the Church have better demonstrated the gift of giving than John Wesley. While he made a point to accept nothing from the regular income of the many Methodist societies under his supervision, he received and gave away many thousands of pounds from his publications. So keenly did he feel at this point that he asked all to condemn him as a thief if he should die with more than a few shillings in his purse.

Not only do givers give out of abundance; the gift of giving leads to joyful but still real sacrifice. Giving is to be generous, and generosity begins only at the point of sacrifice. It is not generous to give what will not be missed. It is not generous to bestow on others what we ourselves will never need.

Probably more Christians have this gift latent within them than almost any other. Certainly, fewer seem to "covet" it than "covet" some of the more spectacular gifts. We could all cultivate it much more than we do. It is still "more blessed to give than to receive" as Paul quoted an otherwise unknown beatitude of Jesus (Acts 20:35). If we are remembered at all, it will not be for what we have received but for what we have given.

## 6. Leadership

Leadership or "ruling" is the next gift on Paul's Romans list. It is literally "taking the lead" in the efforts of a group. Some leaders are no doubt born. Others become leaders in spiritual matters by the endowment of God's Holy Spirit.

The qualifying word in connection with the gift of leadership or administration is "diligently"—with earnestness, zeal, and in a businesslike manner. While leadership may in large part be a function of office or position, the office or position itself may be given in recognition of some promise of administrative ability.

Genuine spiritual leadership is still a crying need in the Church. One of the encouraging features of our day is the growing recognition of the importance of lay leadership in spiritual activities. A generation ago, Dr. J. B. Chapman wrote, "Practically all the spiritual movements of history have been marked by the large place which 'the people' occupied in the services and in the general activities of the Church; and the less spiritual a movement becomes the more completely the pastor and other leaders absorb the time."[3]

Leadership demands vision, patience, consistency of objective, and the strength to carry on when others are will-

33

ing to quit. These are all qualities with a spiritual dimension. The leader must be, as Wilson Lanpher remarked, "both a dreamer and a drummer." He must envision the objectives to be reached, and he must set the pace for those who work with him. Blessed is that church which does not stifle leadership but encourages its people to exercise their gift.

## 7. Compassion

The last of the service gifts listed in Romans is translated "showing mercy." It is compassion or concern—kindness to others. Phillips translates it "feels sympathy." It is that sort of sensitivity to the feelings of others that we would now probably call "empathy," the rare but important power to put oneself in the place of another—to "walk in his mocassins."

It may seem surprising to find listed as a spiritual gift a quality or attitude that is in fact required of all believers. The New Testament repeatedly states that the mercy we receive from God is limited only by the mercy we give. It is the "merciful" who "will be shown mercy" (Matt. 5:7). The chorus is true:

> Except I am moved with compassion,
> How dwelleth Thy Spirit in me?
> In word and in deed,
> Burning love is my need;
> I know I can find it in Thee.

Yet in an age of "dry eyes, hard noses, and cold feet," there is need for specially conspicuous examples of compassion. It is this Paul lists among the gifts of the Spirit. Prayerless tears and tearless prayers are alike unavailing. Compassion is "your ache in my heart." The Holy Spirit never closes our hearts. Rather He tears them open to the needs of those about.

As with all the other gifts, there is genuine joy in the exercise of "showing mercy." There are no rainbows in tearless eyes. In Shakespeare's memorable lines:

> *The quality of mercy is not strain'd,*
> *It droppeth as the gentle rain from heaven*
> *Upon the place beneath. It is twice bless'd:*
> *It blesseth him that gives and him that takes:*
> *'Tis mightiest in the mightiest: it becomes*
> *The throned monarch better than his crown. . . .*
> *It is an attribute to God himself.*

As "contributing to the needs of others" is to be generous, and leadership is to be diligent, so showing mercy is to be done "cheerfully." The word here *(hilarotes)* is used only once in the New Testament. A related adjective *(hilaros)* is also used once—in 2 Cor. 9:7, "God loves a cheerful [*hilaros*] giver." It is the source of the English cognate *hilarious*—certainly the opposite of reluctance, gloominess, a grudging attitude.

There is a gloomy compassion that depresses. What the *charisma* of compassion does is to bring comfort and cheer —not by ignoring the reality of conditions that oppress the one in need of mercy, but by bringing the light of faith and hope to the scene.

# 4

# The Corinthians List

Paul's second major listing of *charismata* is found in 1 Cor. 12:7-11: "Now to each man the manifestation of the Spirit is given for the common good. To one there is given through the Spirit the ability to speak with wisdom, to another the ability to speak with knowledge by means of the same Spirit, to another faith by the same Spirit, to another gifts of healing by that one Spirit, to another miraculous powers, to another the ability to distinguish between spirits, to another the ability to speak in different kinds of languages [fn.], and to still another the interpretation of languages [fn.]."

Some rather striking differences between this and the Romans list are apparent. Only the gift of prophecy is found on both lists, a gift which Paul says in 1 Corinthians 14 he prizes above all others. It has been suggested that the Romans list deals with gifts that are part of the everyday life of the Christian community. On the other hand, the Corinthians list deals with gifts that are more exceptional, more transitory, less universal. The very fact that the lists are so different shows that spiritual gifts cover a far wider range of abilities and powers than we customarily think.

It is possible that the differences between the two lists reflect differences between the two churches to which Paul was writing. The church at Rome seems to have been a very stable and spiritual community. It was unmarred by inner strife or by doctrinal heresy. The apostle honored it with the most thorough treatise on the gospel we have in the New Testament.

The Corinthian church, by contrast, was the problem church of the New Testament. It was split into contending factions (1 Cor. 1:10—3:23); in rebellion against Paul's authority (4:1-21); marred by immorality (5:1-13) and internal lawsuits (6:1-8); its love feasts had deteriorated into times of gluttony and drunkenness (11:18-34); and doctrinal heresies were tolerated, even to the extent of denial of the resurrection of Christ (15:1-58). The situation improved somewhat in the interval between the writing of 1 and 2 Corinthians, but it was still far from stabilized (2 Cor. 13:1-10).

The Corinthians seem to have been enamored with the more specialized and obvious gifts. Paul is concerned that they recognize that, while "there are different kinds of spiritual gifts," all are gifts of the "same Spirit"; "different kinds of service" are rendered to "the same Lord"; there are "different kinds of working, but the same God works all of them in all men" (1 Cor. 12:4-6). All God's gifts are important and none of them is without meaning. But what we are called upon to see is that, while gifts, services, and workings are varied, the Spirit, Lord, and God behind them is the Three-in-One God, who is Spirit, Son, and Father.

## 1. The Ability to Speak with Wisdom

"The ability to speak with wisdom" is the first *charisma* on the Corinthian list. What the KJV translates as "the word of wisdom" is *logos sophias* in the Greek New Testament. Closely paired with it is "the word of knowledge," the second gift.

These first two gifts on the Corinthians list are also closely related to teaching and prophecy or speaking to men to edification, exhortation, and comfort. Jesus taught that the Holy Spirit is to be our Teacher and guide us into all truth (John 14:26; 16:15). He therefore is the Source of all spiritual wisdom and knowledge.

This does not mean that the Holy Spirit acts independently of natural abilities and aptitudes. But natural abilities and aptitudes fall short in the area of spiritual insight and knowledge without these gifts of the Spirit (1 Cor. 2:7-16).

Because of their key importance, "the ability to speak with wisdom" and "the ability to speak with knowledge" are among the most widespread of spiritual gifts. Pastors, Sunday school teachers, youth leaders, members of Bible study groups sharing their insights, laymen in times of testimony—all over the church, men and women who would never think of themselves as gifted persons are speaking "the word of wisdom" and "the word of knowledge."

With regard to "the word of wisdom," both *logos* and *sophia* are terms rich in meaning. *Logos* means, variously, "word, speech, teaching, doctrine, message, communication." *Sophia* is defined as "insight, understanding, judgment, good sense, sanity, ability to grasp the real essence of things—to get at the heart of it," as we would say.

The Bible has much to say about wisdom and man's need for it. "The fear of the Lord is the beginning of wisdom" (Prov. 9:10, KJV). One may have much knowledge—in the sense of the apprehension of facts—without having much wisdom. It is claimed that there are enough Ph.Ds in the average state penitentiary to staff a good-sized college. Much learning has not made them wise. Some, said Peter Forsyth in one of his characteristic paradoxes, "are too clever ever to be very wise."[1]

One modern theologian recalls the remark of an observer at the beginning of the modern scientific movement: "Under the new method science will increase but wisdom will decrease." By wisdom, he meant understanding the principles which determine life and the world. His words were prophetic: science has all but conquered wisdom; knowledge has all but crowded out insight.[2]

Paul's strongest words about wisdom are found in 1 Cor. 1:17—2:16. God has made foolish "the wisdom of the world" (1:20). "The foolishness of God is wiser than man's wisdom, and the weakness of God is stronger than man's strength" (1:25). Christ is "the power of God and the wisdom of God" (1:24); and God's wisdom, impenetrable to the unilluminated mind, is revealed to us by His Spirit (2:6-16).

"Ability to speak with wisdom" is often given to those who are untrained in theological or biblical disciplines. "The word of wisdom" is often spoken by the humble and academically illiterate. Countless multitudes of laymen as well as ministers have blessed Christ's Church through their use of this spiritual gift.

## 2. The Ability to Speak with Knowledge

The second gift on the Corinthian list is "ability to speak with knowledge." This is not tautology. The Greek phrase is *logos gnoseos*. *Gnosis* means the apprehension of facts, recognition of truth, or coming to know. "The power to express knowledge" is one translation; "the ability to speak intelligently" is another.

To grasp and communicate knowledge relates to a large extent to what would be identified as intelligence or mental ability. But the gift here is more than a native intelligence quotient. It is a supernatural heightening of powers of comprehension and communication through the energy of the Holy Spirit.

Just as there is worldly wisdom contrasted with divine wisdom, there is a kind of knowledge that tends to pride. It is the kind of knowledge that "puffs up" (1 Cor. 8:1). The knowledge which is the basis of *logos gnoseos*, on the other hand, is knowledge that ministers to genuine humility. One who shares the knowledge that comes from the Spirit's teaching is aware of how much he doesn't know as well as being sure of what he does.

*Knowledge* and *knowing*—as the terms are used in the Scriptures—always involve personal experience. There is a directness and immediacy about spiritual knowledge that is closely related to intuition. The very Greek word for "I know" is grammatically related to the verb "to see" or "I have seen." The earliest Old Testament name for a prophet was "seer," in the literal sense of "one who sees."

Just as *knowledge* in the biblical use of the term means personal involvement, it also is imparted as an incentive and guide to action—never for mere information alone. Spiritual knowledge is "instrumental"—it is a means to the end that life and service may be pleasing to God.

The ultimate Christian knowledge is to know "the only true God, and Jesus Christ, whom . . . [He has] sent" (John 17:3). In a hauntingly beautiful paragraph, British Scholar Norman Snaith wrote:

> This is a type of certainty which I, for one, have about God. It is not contrary to reason, and given its own premises it is as logical as the rest. But it has its own premises, and they are the premises which have their basis in personal experience of a Person. Nobody ever argued me into it, and I am quite certain that nobody can ever argue me out of it. It never depended on that type of argument. If anyone should ask me how it is that I am sure of God, I could give no answer except that it is in the same kind of way in which I am sure of my wife. Just how it is that I am sure of that, I do not know. It has been strengthened by the intimacies and mutual trust of the years, but it began . . . ? The Christian is prepared to give reasons for the faith that is in him, but his faith does not depend upon such reasons.[3]

40

### 3. Faith

The third *charisma* on the Corinthians list is faith. *Faith* is a word with several meanings in the New Testament. It is used for the obedient trust that is a Christian's response to the gospel. This is not a "gift" in the primary sense—only in the sense that every human capacity is ultimately the gift of God. Eph. 2:8-9 has sometimes been interpreted to mean that saving faith itself is God's direct gift, "For it is by grace you have been saved, through faith—and this not from yourselves, it is the gift of God—not by works, so that no one can boast." But the meaning here is that *grace* is the gift of God. Through saving faith we receive the grace-gift of eternal life (Rom. 6:23).

*Faith* is also used to describe the requirement to receive God's gift of a pure heart. Peter reported on the baptism with the Spirit that came on Cornelius and his family, "God, who knows the heart, showed that he accepted them by giving the Holy Spirit to them, just as he did to us. He made no distinction between us and them, for he purified their hearts *by faith*" (Acts 15:8-9). Christ gave Paul his mission to the Gentiles: "I am sending you to open their eyes and turn them from darkness to light, and from the power of Satan to God, so that they may receive forgiveness of sins and a place among those who are sanctified *by faith in me*" (Acts 26:16-18, italics added).

*Faith* is also used in the sense of "faithfulness," or dependability. This is its meaning in Gal. 5:22-23, where the fruit of the Spirit is described as including "faithfulness, gentleness and self-control."

But faith as a gift of the Spirit is none of these. It is rather faith of the kind Jesus described in Matt. 17:20—"faith as small as a mustard seed"—a faith that can remove mountains of difficulty. All over the Church, people whose names may never appear in a directory of outstanding spiritual leaders are exercising the gift of faith as they face the challenge of their circumstances.

The gift of faith is involved in extraordinary answers to prayer. Basic Christian faith is generated by the Word of God. Faith for the extraordinary comes as the direct gift of the Spirit. Achieving faith is indeed one of the "greater gifts" we each may well "eagerly desire" (1 Cor. 12:30).

Two final points may be made about the gift of faith:

*a.* In one sense, faith underlies all *charismata.* This is indicated in Rom. 12:3, 6, where Paul speaks of "the measure of faith God has given" to each, and speaks of using the gift of prophecy "in proportion to his faith."

*b.* Closely related is the implication that all in some degree may exercise the gift of faith and should be encouraged to. Remembering that achieving faith is not given to get for us what we want but what God wants us to have, we may still profit by William Carey's well-known injunction: "Expect great things from God; attempt great things for God."

> *If our faith were but more simple,*
> *We would take Him at His word;*
> *And our lives would be all sunshine*
> *In the sweetness of our Lord.*

### 4. Gifts of Healings

This fourth gift on the Corinthians list has been widely misunderstood. Most of the English translations, including the NIV, miss the obvious fact in the original that in all three references here (1 Cor. 12:9, 28, 30), both "gifts" *(charismata)* and "healings" *(iamaton),* are plural. This is no generalized "gift of healing" that can be exercised in favor of any and all who come. These are specific gifts for specific instances of healing.

Paul here is in direct accord with Jas. 5:14-15, "Is any one of you sick? He should call the elders of the church to pray over [not *above*, but *about*] him and anoint him with oil in the name of the Lord. And the prayer offered in faith will make the sick person well; the Lord will raise him up." The point appears to be that faith for a specific healing will be given (or withheld) when believers pray about the need before them.

Paul is also in accord with the experience of the Church throughout the ages in his emphasis on "gifts of healings." That miraculous and medically inexplicable cures have and. do take place in undeniable. That healing is sometimes withheld is equally undeniable.

Few have been more liberally endowed with gifts of healings than the Apostle Paul himself. Yet at times they were unavailable to him. He left Trophimus, a cherished co-worker, sick at Miletus (2 Tim. 4:20). He urged Timothy to take care of a weak stomach (1 Tim. 5:23). He prayed three times concerning his own "thorn in the flesh"—almost certainly a physical affliction—and received a larger blessing than physical healing, the sufficient grace of Christ (2 Cor. 12:7-10).

That there are gifts of healings does not mean that the dedicated work of doctors and nurses is to be spurned. Only fanaticism would refuse available and helpful medication. The devout Christian recognizes all healing as the work of God, even though a poultice of figs be applied (Isa. 38:21) and oil and wine be poured into the wounds (Luke 10:34). The father of modern surgery, Ambroise Paré, is reported to have said, "I tended him; God healed him." God heals through creation, the ways of which we are just beginning to learn, as well as through Christ.

"Gifts of healings" are given and used throughout the Church in many unobtrusive ways. We must not, in E. Stanley Jones's words, "allow the queer to queer it for us." There are counterfeits and frauds and the exploitation of human suffering in "deliverance revivals" advertising the

43

filling of teeth and hanging crutches and wheelchairs from tent poles. But there is also a large and growing circle of devout Christians who are preaching and practicing divine healing. Many are from so-called "old-line churches"— Episcopal, Methodist, Presbyterian, for example. Outstanding is Rev. Dr. Alfred Price, whose weekly service for divine healing in St. Stephen's Episcopal Church in downtown Philadelphia has become an established institution with an unquestionable record of good results. The Order of St. Luke the Physician is composed of doctors, ministers, and laymen largely from the traditional churches and dedicated to the ministry of healing within the church.

This is all to the good. We need to recognize that physical healing is not something "tacked on" to the gospel. It is an authentic part of God's plan to meet all our human need according to His will. We have a real challenge to take seriously and emphasize more what has always been part of our heritage. We should preach, practice, believe in, and call for the ministry of divine healing.

We should do this, not as bait to trap the otherwise unconcerned, nor as a hook for the curious or sensation-seeker, but as a true and important part of the provision of God in Christ to supply all our needs according to His riches in glory. In the exercise of prayer, faith, and obedience, "gifts of healings" are given for the glory of God the Father.

### 5. Miraculous Powers

"Working of miracles" (KJV) is the fifth *charisma* on the Corinthians list. The Greek phrase is *energemata dunameon*. *Energeia* is the obvious source of our English word *energy*, and *dunamis* is the root of *dynamo* and *dynamite*. The KJV translators used such English words as "ability, abundance, deed, might, miracle, power, strength, and work" to translate *dunamis*. They translated *energeia* as "working, operation."

*Dunamis* throughout the New Testament is used to describe results that could not be produced by natural agents or means. There were many miracles of a physical sort in the New Testament. Many of these were obviously regarded as signs or evidences authenticating the mission of Christ and the apostles. John, for example, describes the turning of water into wine as *archen ton semion* ("beginning of miracles," KJV), literally, "the beginning of the signs" (John 2:1-11); and throughout the fourth Gospel, Christ's miracles are consistently defined as "signs" (2:11, 23; 3:2; 4:54; 6:2, 14, 26; 7:31; 9:16; 11:47; 12, 37; 20:30).

While authenticating signs are no longer necessary or given (Heb. 2:4, note the past tense), miraculous powers are still given in the Church. One can have little patience with the kind of emphasis on the miraculous that results in the "Can you top this?" sort of anecdote. Claiming to fill teeth and lengthen the legs of people who have never walked with a limp is nothing but "Mickey Mouse" compared with the power that transforms lives.

But all over the Church and all the time, results are occurring for which no solely human cause is apparent. Genuine miracles are not only physical but psychological and spiritual. The minds and dispositions of people are changed as God works miracles in human lives. Gal. 3:5 extends the use of the term *miracle* to transformations of character in what are really and truly "miracles of grace." It took a miracle "to hang the stars in space." It takes a greater miracle to bring order into the chaos of a disordered life (2 Cor. 4:6) and bring about a new creation (2 Cor. 5:17).

### 6. Prophecy

*Propheteia*—speaking "to men for their strengthening,

encouragement and comfort"—is, as we have noted, the one gift common to both the Romans and the Corinthians lists. The addition made in the Corinthian correspondence is Paul's estimate of this as the highest or most desirable of all gifts (1 Cor. 12:31; 14:1). The gift itself was discussed in connection with the *charismata* listed in Romans 12.

## 7. The Ability to Distinguish Between Spirits

"Discerning of spirits" is the KJV translation of *diakriseis pneumaton*. *Diakrisis* means "decision, separating, discriminating, determining"—all of which are aspects of discernment. *Pneuma* is the regular Greek word for *breath*, *wind*, *spirit*, or *Spirit*, and is also translated "life" and "spiritual" in some contexts in the KJV. "The ability to distinguish between spirits" is Paul's title for the gift Christians use when they heed John's words: "Dear friends, do not believe every spirit, but test the spirits to see whether they are from God, because many false prophets have gone out into the world" (1 John 4:1).

There is probably a reason why Paul places "ability to distinguish between spirits" next to his listing of the last two *charismata* on the Corinthians table. The modern confusion over language gifts—pro and con—is abundant reason for the need for extraordinary powers of discernment. The KJV translation of Prov. 25:14 sounds an important warning: "Whoso boasteth himself of a false gift is like clouds and wind without rain." It is the discernment of spirits that enables us to distinguish between the working of the human spirit and the working of the divine Spirit.

## 8. Different Kinds of Languages

The eighth *charisma* on Paul's Corinthians list is *gene glosson*, "divers kinds of tongues" (KJV), "different kinds of tongues" (NIV), or "different kinds of languages" (NIV and fn.).

We have used the term "languages" instead of the more familiar "tongues" for a reason. In our day and time, the English word *tongues* has become so identified with the practice of "unknown tongues" that it is almost impossible for us to escape this connotation. Yet *tongues* in 1611, when the KJV was translated, meant just what we now mean by *languages*. Jesus spoke to Paul on the road to Damascus in the Hebrew tongue or language (Acts 26:14), and when Paul addressed the mob in Jerusalem he spoke to them in "the Hebrew tongue" or language (Acts 21:40, KJV). John saw a great multitude in heaven "of all nations, and kindreds, and people, and tongues" or languages (Rev. 7:9, KJV).

### 9. The Interpretation of Languages

The companion gift to different kinds of languages is "the interpretation of tongues" or "the interpretation of languages" (NIV and fn.). The Greek phrase is *hermeneia glosson. Hermeneia,* from which we get *hermeneutics,* means "interpretation or translation." It means to give the sense of speech in one language in another, to translate meaning from one language to another.

Because of the wide interest in the language gifts, particularly speaking in "other tongues," we shall look more extensively at these in the following chapter. However, putting the service gifts together from both the Romans and Corinthians lists, we get a marvelous overview of the abilities necessary for the complete functioning of the body of Christ:

1. Speaking for edification, exhortation, and comfort for others

2. Service—ministering to human needs

3. Teaching—grounding others in the truth

4. Exhortation or encouragement—stimulating faith in others

5. Giving or sharing with generosity

6. Leadership—taking the lead in joint efforts with others

7. Compassion or concern—empathy

8. Speaking with wisdom

9. Ability to grasp and communicate knowledge

10. Mustard-seed faith

11. Gifts of healings

12. Miracles, especially miracles of grace

13. Discernment of spirits

14. Different kinds of languages

15. Interpretation of languages

Each of us may note with gratitude the gifts that have been working in our lives. Each of us may well "eagerly desire the greater gifts" (1 Cor. 12:31) that we do not as yet see working in us, or working in as large a measure as our circumstances and responsibilities demand. While the sovereign Spirit has reserved to himself the final distribution of His gifts, He encourages us to desire those most important.

**5**

# The Language Gifts

No apology is necessary for a more extended look at the language gifts in the New Testament. The amount of space given here is admittedly greater than the ranking of these gifts in Paul's estimation would normally warrant. But the emphasis of this century on this particular aspect of the charismata not only justifies but demands a full consideration of what is involved in "speaking in tongues."

One point must be made in a preliminary way. For many years the author taught college courses in logic—the principles and practice of correct thinking. Among the fallacies that threaten clear thinking is the fallacy of attempting to refute a theory by attacking the motives or judging the character of those who hold that theory. This is known technically as "the *argumentum ad hominem.*" It is always wrong.

There is a companion error. It is the fallacy of supposing that to discuss a theory means a personal attack on those who hold that theory. Nothing could be farther from the truth. Christians may be better than their creeds—or, on the other hand, not as good. In either case, the creed may be examined—even critically, if necessary—without implying any criticism of the life and character of the person who holds that creed.

In considering the language gifts, it is impossible to avoid differences of interpretation. To the extent to which one must differ with warmhearted and sincere Christian brothers and sisters who hold other theologies, it must always be regarded as a lovers' quarrel.

We should carry no cudgels and throw no stones at those whose worship of the Lord differs from our own. Nor should we ignore the issues differing theories create. All of us must test our theories by scripture. The Bible must be given first place in matters of faith and practice. What we must try to do is to find out for ourselves "what saith the Lord."

## I. GLOSSOLALIA

Just as *charismatic* has made its way from New Testament Greek into the religious vocabulary of our day, so has the term *glossolalia*. *Glossa* means both "the tongue" in the literal sense of the organ of speech in the mouth, and, as we have already seen, "language." *Lalein* is "to speak." Hence, *glossolalia* has come to be the technical term used to describe "speaking in tongues." While the term is popularly extended to the use of unlearned foreign languages, these are technically known as *xenoglossa*. The typical and more careful use of the term *glossolalia* describes speaking a language which neither the speaker nor the hearer understands unless endowed with a parallel gift of interpretation.[1]

The contemporary Christian faces two issues regarding *glossolalia*. One is the theological or doctrinal interpretation given to it—that speaking in tongues is the necessary, initial, biblical evidence of the baptism with the Holy Spirit. The other is the system of piety that has grown up around the idea of unknown tongues as a special language of prayer and praise.

Both of these issues raise serious and even crucial questions. These questions can never be answered by multiplying testimonials, either "for" or "against." They can be settled only by considering the full teaching of the Scriptures. Experience may confirm but it cannot control biblical interpretation. The Word of God must have decisive authority in all matters that pertain to the Christian life.

## II. THE PENTECOSTAL CLAIM

The present emphasis on glossolalia is strictly a twentieth-century development. The claim that this gift is of central importance and is the essential initial physical evidence of the fullness of the Spirit was first proposed by Charles F. Parham in connection with the occurrence of glossolalia in 1901 in his small Bible school in Topeka, Kans.

There had been prior instances of glossolalia recorded, both Christian and non-Christian. The heretical Montanists in the early Christian centuries, the Albigenses in Italy, the Port Royal Jansenists in France, the Irvingites in nineteenth-century England, and the Mormons and Shakers in the United States all practiced glossolalia. But no theological conclusion had been drawn from the practice. The most recent historian of the Pentecostal movement in the United States credits Parham with being "the father of modern Pentecostalism."[2]

There is, on the face of it, reason to suspect any fundamental theological novelty. Theology may indeed increase its understanding of scripture and God's ways with men. But such understanding in no way alters the basic truths of the gospel. John Wesley's well-known dictum is correct: In Christian faith, whatever is new is not true, and whatever is true is not new.

What do we find in the Bible when we look at present-day claims for *glossolalia?*

51

## III. Indirect Evidence

There is first what might be called the indirect evidence of the Bible at this point. Languages first appear in the Bible as barriers to separate men from each other. At the Tower of Babel (Genesis 11), different languages were part of God's judgment on the sinful pride of man. The widely diverse human languages of today had their beginnings as a result of what happened at Babel, a word which itself has come to mean unintelligible speech.

Later in the Old Testament, all the essential characteristics of the age of the Spirit are freely foretold without any mention of languages or tongues in connection with it. Isaiah, Ezekiel, Joel, Zechariah, and Malachi speak of the fruitfulness and blessing, the fiery cleansing, the freedom in prayer, the law of God reinforced in the soul, and the grace and vision which were to come. But they breathe no word of an essential physical sign or evidence such as glossolalia is said to be.

Isa. 28:11 is not an exception to this statement: "For with stammering lips and another tongue will he speak to this people" (KJV). This verse, quoted in 1 Cor. 14:21, has clear reference to the judgments about to fall on Ephraim at the hands of the Assyrians and later the Babylonians, whose speech seemed stammering and whose languages were strange. This passage has important bearing on our understanding of 1 Corinthians 14.

Indirect evidence in the New Testament is also significant. John the Baptist gave the first word in the New Testament about the soon coming baptism with the Spirit. His contrast between his own water baptism and the baptism with the Holy Spirit which Christ was to administer is given in all four Gospels (Matt. 3:11-12; Mark 1:7-8; Luke 3:16-17; John 1:33). It was quoted by Jesus (Acts 1:5) and by Peter (Acts 11:16). Yet John made no mention whatever of an initial physical sign that the baptism had been accomplished.

It is noteworthy that Jesus Christ, to whom the Father gave the Spirit without measure (John 3:34), is nowhere said to have spoken any other language than the native Aramaic of Palestine.

More than any other in the New Testament, Jesus gave the definitive doctrine of the Holy Spirit in His great "Paraclete" sayings in the Last Supper Discourse (John 14—16). Yet nowhere did He mention any confirming linguistic sign. No doctrine can be considered essential or even important in Christianity that does not have its roots in the teachings of Jesus himself.

On one occasion at least, the disciples asked Jesus to teach them to pray (Luke 11:1). His reply said nothing about a "prayer language" that would more effectively express their desires to God than could their ordinary speech. He taught them to pray in the clear, lucid, and completely understandable words of "The Lord's Prayer" (vv. 2-4).

The single reference in Mark's Gospel to "new tongues" is found in a section of the Gospel missing from the most reliable early manuscripts (16:9-20). Even so, the new tongues have no reference to the baptism with the Spirit. They refer to one of the general signs that will "accompany those who believe"—a list that includes taking up serpents and drinking poison without harm. The words "those who believe" relate the passage to saving faith in general, not an explicit baptism with the Holy Spirit. It is only fair to say in addition that "new tongues" are not necessarily "unknown tongues."

It should be admitted that the "argument from silence" is by no means conclusive. Neither is it unimportant. If Jesus, by example and in teaching, stressed the baptism or fullness of the Spirit without a single word about other languages, such could hardly be the only valid, initial physical evidence of that baptism or essential to Christian piety. Whatever is of major importance to Christian faith and practice is a consistent note throughout all scripture and most certainly in the teachings of Jesus.

# IV. DIRECT EVIDENCE

Direct evidence concerning glossolalia is found in two books: Acts and 1 Corinthians.

## 1. In the Book of Acts

The Book of Acts is a record of the experience of the Early Church, both at the beginning of the age of the Spirit and in its ongoing.

The impression is sometimes given that speaking in tongues was a universal phenomenon in the beginning days of Christianity. An examination of the Book of Acts reveals only three instances of speaking in unlearned languages, and these widely separated in time and place. The first was in Jerusalem on the first Christian Day of Pentecost (Acts 2). The second was some five years later in Caesarea (Acts 10). The third was in Ephesus, approximately 19 years later still (Acts 19). The record, at least, fails to show any widespread practice of or preoccupation with the language speaking involved.

Another point in the chronology of the New Testament has bearing here. Although we read Acts before we read 1 Corinthians, the Corinthian letter was written some eight or nine years *before* the Book of Acts. Luke was the author of Acts and the longtime companion and "beloved physician" of the Apostle Paul. There is little doubt that he was the person sent to Corinth by Paul as mentioned in 2 Cor. 8:18. Both his close association with Paul and firsthand acquaintance with the church in Corinth would certainly make him familiar with the conditions described in 1 Corinthians 14 related to the practice of tongues.

In the light of this, Luke's description of the languages at Pentecost assumes crucial importance. In Acts 2, Luke carefully lists the languages spoken (vv. 9-11) and twice mentions the amazement of the assembled crowd that the people there heard "each" one "in his own native language" (v. 8) "the wonders of God"—and it is stated again, "in our own tongues" (v. 11). This may very well be Luke's way of saying to all who might have heard of the phenomenon at Corinth, "This is what the New Testament gift of languages *really* is."

In any case, there is little doubt about the nature of the phenomenon at the Jerusalem Pentecost. It was the Spirit-inspired capacity to speak God's wonderful works in languages the apostles had not learned but which were perfectly understood by people who knew those languages.

Was the miracle of languages at Pentecost a miracle of speaking or a miracle of hearing? Certainly, Luke seems to assume that the disciples were actually speaking the languages and dialects of the areas listed. But whether the miracle was one of hearing or speaking, it was surely a miracle of communication. There was speaking that was understood by those who heard without any interpretation.

There were therefore no *"unknown* tongues at Pentecost. In fact the gift that was given there was for the very purpose of preventing unknown tongues. The native language of the Galilean disciples (Acts 2:7) was a distinctive form of Aramaic easily recognized by those living in other parts of Palestine (Matt. 26:73). But the Parthians, Medes, Elamites, Mesopotamians, Judeans, Cappadocians, and men of Pontus, Asia, Phrygia, Pamphylia, Egypt, Libya, Rome, Crete, and Arabia all heard in their native dialects. If the disciples had spoken in *their* own native language, they would have been speaking a tongue unknown to multitudes in that cosmopolitan crowd.

There is no indication in Acts that the gift at Pentecost was a permanent power given for extended missionary purposes. It was indeed a sign—not to believers that they were filled with the Spirit, but as Paul said concerning the practice of tongues in Corinth, "a sign . . . for unbelievers" (1 Cor. 14:22) that the gospel there announced was in fact for all men everywhere, whatever their languages might be.

Here was an eloquent testimony that God was reversing what had been brought about by man's sinful pride at Babel. It was a sign for all ages of the breaking down of the barriers between nations through Christ and His gospel. It was a striking witness to the universality of the gospel message, to men of every tongue and in every clime.

If today, as has been reported, there are instances of persons actually speaking other languages, there would be no reason to deny the work of God. But speech which neither the speaker nor anyone else can understand unless he has a parallel gift of interpretation is far from the miracle of Pentecost. To identify the languages of Pentecost and "unknown tongues" is to fly in the face of both reason and scripture and can result only in utter confusion.

The other two instances in the Acts of the Apostles where languages were spoken (Acts 10; 19) are not described in detail. There would be no reason to suppose that the phenomenon was any different from that described in Acts 2. Indeed, in the case of Cornelius, the disciples with Peter are said in the literal wording of the Greek New Testament to have "heard them speaking languages and glorifying God" (Acts 10:46), implying that they were understood. In a similar way, the Ephesian disciples "spoke languages and prophesied" (Acts 19:6, lit.), again implying that the content of the speaking was recognized.

Indeed, in the case of Cornelius, if the language gift were in any sense an evidence of the baptism with the Holy Spirit, Peter's silence about it in his two reports on the occurrence (Acts 11 and 15) becomes inexplicable. The point of issue when Peter reported back to the Jerusalem church (Acts 11) and later at the council in Jerusalem (Acts 15) was whether or not the Gentiles had indeed received the fullness of the Spirit. Peter had but to mention the language phenomenon to make the case, if indeed tongues were an evidence. He mentioned it not all, resting his case on the fact that the Holy Spirit "purified their hearts by faith" (Acts 15:8-9).

It will be noted that the three instances of speaking in tongues recorded in Acts all occurred at crucial watershed times in the advance of the gospel.

At Pentecost, the gospel broke out beyond the bounds of Palestinian Judaism to embrace devout men from the Dispersion living all over the Mediterranean world.

In Caesarea, the gospel moved beyond the circle of birthright Jews to include Gentile proselytes.

In Ephesus, the gospel transcended all limits of race or previous connection with Judaism and included those converted out of raw paganism.

In each of these instances, there were persons of different nationalities and linguistic backgrounds present. Speaking other languages was the most natural possible sign that a major breakthrough had occurred.

The evidence of Acts is not complete until the many instances are considered in which there is reference to the fullness of the Spirit or receiving the Spirit in connection with which there is no allusion, direct or indirect, to speaking in tongues. These include Acts 1:5, 8; 4:8, 31; 5:32; 6:3, 5; 8:15, 17-19; 9:17; 11:15-16, 24; 13:9, 52; and 15:8.

## 2. Tongues in Corinth

When we turn back from the Book of Acts to the Corinthian correspondence, we immediately run into difficulties in interpretation. Of the nature of the language speaking in Acts, there is little reasonable doubt. It involved the use of foreign languages in contexts where they were recognized and understood without any interpretation. There was, in all of this, no hint of an "unknown" tongue which neither the speaker nor the hearers understand unless gifted with a parallel *charisma* of interpretation. Actually the terms *charisma* and *charismata* are not used in the Book of Acts.

Only in Corinth is there a New Testament record of the use or abuse of a language gift. As we have seen, Paul's list of *charismata* in Romans 12 makes no mention of speaking in tongues. Nor does any other New Testament writer.

This in itself creates problems of interpretation. As we have seen, the Corinthian church was a seriously troubled church. It was the least exemplary of all the churches described in the New Testament, not excepting even the churches of Galatia. Yet only in Corinth is there any indication of speaking in tongues.

A second difficulty in interpreting the data lies in the sharp and almost complete divergence of opinion among equally learned and devout Bible scholars as to the exact nature of what was happening at Corinth.

One major view is that the languages of Corinth were like those at Jerusalem—human languages spoken under the direct and immediate inspiration of the Holy Spirit. While such languages were not always understood in Corinth, they would have been intelligible to any who might have known the languages spoken.

Scholars of this persuasion would argue that just as we should interpret the symbolism of Revelation in the light of the clear statements of the Gospels and the Epistles rather than vice versa, so we should interpret 1 Corinthians—particularly chapter 14—in the light of Acts 2 rather than vice versa.

The other major view, widely accepted in this century, is that the tongues of Corinth were ecstatic utterances meaningless to both those who spoke and those who heard, unless there was a corresponding gift of interpretation.

Liberal scholars who interpret the tongues of Corinth as truly "unknown" tend to do so on the assumption that the Corinthian Christians had brought into the church the practices they observed or had experienced in some of the mystery religions of the first century where unknown tongues were spoken. A number of conservative scholars, both outside and within the orbit of Pentecostal practice, regard unknown tongues as a genuine gift of the Holy Spirit.

Some of the difference of opinion as to what was actually going on in Corinth comes from the possibility that both other languages and unknown tongues were to be found there. In part, this may be indicated by the difference in tone and terminology between chapters 12 and 14, as well as by Paul's restraint in chapter 14 in dealing with what he obviously regarded as a troublesome situation.

In 1 Cor. 12:1, Paul announced his intention of dealing with the whole broad subject of *pneumatika*, a term whose distinctive meaning is hidden when it is translated "spiritual gifts" (KJV), as if it were the word *charismata*. *Pneumatika* are literally "spirituals" or spiritual phenomena. The immediate reference in vv. 2-3 to the Gentile worship of dumb idols and the possibility that a person might call Jesus cursed under the domination of other than the Spirit of God indicates that *pneumatika* include both true and false gifts.

Throughout the balance of chapter 12, Paul deals theologically with the entire range of the more spectacular *charismata* as true gifts of the Spirit (vv. 4-31). His emphasis, as we have seen, is both on the diversity of the gifts and the unity of their source and effects.

Christians are to "covet earnestly the best gifts" (v. 31, KJV); "and yet," says Paul, "shew I unto you a more excellent way." That "more excellent way" is more than a mere transition from chapter 12 to chapter 14. It is the rule and test of love by which every attainment or alleged gift is to be judged.

Paul applies the test of love to four of the gifts he named in chapter 12. He begins with the last but most controversial, tongues. He also includes prophecy, knowledge, and faith. In addition he compares the understanding of all mysteries, the ultimate in generosity, and martyrdom itself with the surpassing excellence of love (13:1-3). Whether as pseudo-gifts or as gifts retained when grace is lost, all may be possessed or practiced without the Holy Spirit's presence at all—for "God has poured out his love into our hearts by the Holy Spirit, whom he has given us" (Rom. 5:5). He who does not have love does not have the Holy Spirit.

Love alone never fails. Again Paul picks out three of the *charismata* to indicate that their function is at best a temporal and human value. Prophecies will fail; tongues will cease; knowledge shall "vanish away" (v. 8, KJV). Knowledge and prophecy represent the partial. When the perfect has been realized, the partial will cease. The speech and understanding of childhood gives way to the maturity of manhood (vv. 9-11). At best we see in or through a glass that tends to distort reality. But there is coming a time when we shall see face-to-face and know as we are known (v. 12). Three transcending values abide: faith, hope, and love. But the greatest of these is love (v. 13).

## V. 1 Corinthians 14

The theological foundation is firmly laid and the principle stated that all must be judged in the light of God's kind of love in 1 Corinthians 12 and 13. Paul then proceeds to deal with some of the practical problems he sees in the Corinthian church.

In 1 Corinthians 14, the apostle deals administratively with one of the critical issues in an ailing church. It must be recognized that an entire chapter is devoted to glossolalia, not because it was such a blessing, but because it was such a problem.

### 1. Differences from 1 Corinthians 12

Some striking differences are to be noted between chapters 12 and 14. In the first place, the term *charismata*, used five times in chapter 12, does not occur at all in chapter 14. Instead, Paul reverts to the term *pneumatika*, the inclusive term with which he began the discussion in 12:1 (14:1) and which includes both true and false manifestations.

Second, the Holy Spirit, mentioned 10 times in chapter 12, is not mentioned even once in chapter 14, as the small *s* in verses 2, 14, 15, and 16 correctly indicates.

Third, the word *unknown* does not occur anywhere here in the Greek New Testament. This is shown by the use of italics in most printings of the King James Version. The KJV uses italics, not to emphasize a word as in current practice, but to indicate a word added by the translators for which there is no corresponding term in the original. There is abundant reason to believe that the adjective "unfamiliar" as used in the Berkeley Version margin would be much more appropriate here.

Fourth, whatever it was that was happening in Corinth, Paul was not happy about it. He was not writing to encourage but to correct. He establishes controls he would never impose on a direct and immediate manifestation of the Holy Spirit.

It is possible that some of our puzzles in understanding chapter 14 come from Paul's knowledge that there were in Corinth both the genuine and the human imitations. Some were speaking languages educated people would have understood should they come into the company. The thrice repeated use of "unlearned" to describe those who would be mystified (vv. 16, 23-24, KJV) would appear to show this. Others may have been expressing religious emotions in vocal utterances they did not understand themselves and which were meaningless to others unless interpreted.

Further, it is just as mistaken to set up chapter 14 as a pattern for normal Christian devotions, public or private, as it is to set up Romans 7 as the normal Christian experience. The norm for Christian devotion is found in 1 Corinthians 13, just as the norm for Christian experience is found in Romans 8.

## 2. Unknown or Unfamiliar Languages?

The biblical evidence is too scanty and some of it too ambiguous to permit excessive dogmatism as to whether the utterances of Corinth were indeed unknown tongues or unfamiliar languages. However, it is perfectly possible to read the entire fourteenth chapter of 1 Corinthians as relating to the use of unfamiliar rather than unknown languages.

The context throughout 1 Corinthians 14 is public worship within a specified circle. When in such a circle one speaks in an unfamiliar language, no man present understands him and he speaks only to God. "In spirit [there is no definite article *the* here in the Greek New Testament] he speaketh mysteries" (v. 2, KJV). "Mysteries" are defined in Col. 1:26 as truths revealed in the gospel.

Such speaking edifies the person who speaks (v. 4), a

statement that could hardly apply to utterance the speaker does not understand.

When Paul says, "I would that ye all spake with tongues, but rather that ye prophesied [spoke to men to edification, exhortation, and comfort]" (v. 5, KJV), he is not taking back what he had said in 12:30—"All do not speak with tongues, do they?" No such contradiction is stated. Verse 5 is the familiar New Testament form of comparison, in which alternatives are stated as absolutes. Jesus said in John 6:27, "Labour not for the meat which perisheth, but for that meat which endureth unto everlasting life" (KJV). He was not forbidding us to work for our daily bread. He was simply indicating the lesser value of food for the physical body as compared with food for the soul. Paul told Timothy to "stop drinking only water, and use a little wine because of your stomach and your frequent illnesses" (1 Tim. 5:23). He was not forbidding the drinking of water. He was comparing, in Timothy's case, the often polluted water of the ancient world with the medicinal use of a *little* wine.

Since speaking in understandable languages is essential to the profit of those who hear, Paul stresses the surpassing value of "words easy to be understood" (vv. 6-9, KJV). There are, to be sure, "all sorts of languages in the world" (v. 10). Paul says, "If then I do not grasp the meaning of what someone is saying, I am a foreigner to the speaker, and he is a foreigner to me" (v. 11).

Since the Corinthians are zealous for *pneumatika*, they should seek in all things the edifying of the church. Those who speak languages not generally understood should pray that they may interpret or translate them. It is common experience that people who are fluent in one language may be very halting and limited when they try to express themselves in a second language.

Verses 14 and 15 have been the source of a great deal

of "mytheology." It has been assumed that Paul said, "If I pray in an unknown tongue, my spirit prays, but my mind does not comprehend what I am saying." It is assumed that the word translated "unfruitful" (Greek, *akarpos*) means "uncomprehending" or "unable to understand." But this is not at all what the word means. *Akarpos* means "without fruit," "furnishing nothing to others."[3] Kenneth Wuest translates the phrase, "My intellect confers no benefit upon others."[4] It is not that the speaker in an unfamiliar language does not understand what he says. Rather, his understanding does not help anyone else.

Therefore, Paul wrote, "So what shall I do? I will pray with my spirit, but I will also pray with my mind; I will sing with my spirit, but I will also sing with my mind" (v. 15). In this context, such words can only mean, "Whenever I pray or sing, it will be in such terms as can be understood."

The typical charismatic understanding of vv. 14-15 presupposes a division between *nous* (mind, understanding) and *pneuma* (spirit) that is quite unscriptural. Mind and spirit are not represented in the Bible as separable functions. The human psyche is an indivisible unity. "Spirit, soul and body" (1 Thess. 5:23) and "heart," "soul," "mind," and "strength" (Mark 12:30) are expressions of totality or completeness, not catalogues of separable parts or functions.

Nor does the Holy Spirit act in man apart from his *nous* or mind. It is "the mind controlled by the Spirit" which "is life and peace" (Rom. 8:6). It is by "the renewing of your mind" (Rom. 12:2) and in "the spirit of your mind" (Eph. 4:23, KJV) that the transforming work of the Spirit is carried on. The high goal of Christian aspiration is that "this mind be in you, which was also in Christ Jesus" (Phil. 2:5, KJV). The Holy Spirit himself is the Spirit "of power, and of love, and of a sound mind" (2 Tim. 1:7, KJV).

Paul's concern about the use of intelligible speech is that any in the company who are "unlearned" (KJV) may be able to say, "Amen," in respect to what they hear. This word "unlearned" is repeated twice again in vv. 23 and 24: "If therefore the whole church be come together into one place, and all speak with tongues [unfamiliar languages], and there come in those that are unlearned, or unbelievers, will they not say that ye are mad? But if all prophesy, and there come in one that believeth not, or one unlearned, he is convinced of all, he is judged of all" (KJV).

There would seem to be only one reason why the "unlearned" should be singled out in this way. It is because one who was educated would have at least a chance of recognizing one or more of the languages spoken. Uneducated believers as well as unbelievers need to hear prophecy (speaking "to men for their strengthening, encouragement and comfort," v. 3), not unfamiliar speech. Such persons would profit nothing, and unbelievers would conclude that Christians were crazy, if they heard speaking they could not comprehend.

Verse 18 is another verse that has proved confusing as translated: "I thank God that I speak in tongues more than all of you." A better translation would be "I thank God I speak more languages than you all." Exactly the same term translated "more" *(mallon)* is used in Gal. 4:27:

> "Be glad, O barren woman,
>    who bears no children;
> break forth and cry aloud,
>    you who have no labor pains;
> there are more children of the desolate woman
>    than of her who has a husband."

Here the meaning is clearly "more in number" and not more in degree.

Even though skilled in other languages, Paul stated that he would rather "speak five intelligible words to instruct others than ten thousand words in a tongue" (v. 19).

There is one clear reference in this chapter to human languages. "In the law it is written, With men of other tongues [*heterais glossais*, the exact wording of Acts 2:4] and other lips will I speak unto this people" (v. 21, KJV). Both Isa. 28:11-12, which Paul quotes, and Acts 2:4 show that these languages were languages uncommon in Palestine but not "unknown." The Isaiah passage is a reference to Assyrian and Babylonian conquests of the land. The people refused to hear their prophets speaking languages they could understand. They would therefore hear the word of judgment in the unfamiliar speech of their conquerors.

Paul further says, "Tongues, then, are a sign, not for believers but for unbelievers" (v. 22). As we saw in connection with Acts 2, speaking the gospel in unfamiliar languages has no value as a sign to believers that they are filled with the Holy Spirit. It is for those who do not believe—that the gospel is for them as well as for those who bring the word and whose native language is a foreign tongue. To make speaking in tongues an evidence to believers of the baptism with the Spirit is exactly to reverse Paul's statement.

The apostle also makes it clear that the speaking which was causing so much trouble among the Corinthians was not necessarily the immediate inspiration of the Holy Spirit. It is hardly credible that he would presume to limit or curtail the expression of the Holy Spirit. Rather, he says, "The spirits of prophets are subject to the control of prophets" (v. 32). What originates in the human spirit must be controlled by the human spirit, "for God is not a God of disorder but of peace" (v. 33).

Attention is often called to Paul's injunction in the usual translation of v. 39, "Wherefore, brethren, covet to prophesy, and forbid not to speak with tongues" (KJV). Yet Paul himself *does* forbid speaking in tongues (or unfamiliar languages) if two or at the most three have already spoken

(v. 27), if there is no interpreter present (v. 28), or if the would-be speaker is a woman (v. 34).

It would appear, therefore, that the translation of Paul's words in v. 39 is in error. As it stands, it is in almost direct contradiction to everything that has been said. No one in Corinth was disposed to forbid speaking unfamiliar languages. It appears to have been a status symbol among these young Christians. The word translated "forbid" normally means "hinder." A translation that would unify the whole passage is: "Therefore, my brothers, be eager to prophesy, and do not hinder by speaking in tongues. Everything should be done in a fitting and orderly way" (vv. 39-40).[5]

Much more might be said, but it should at least be evident that there is nothing in the New Testament to warrant the doctrine that speaking in unknown tongues is the essential, initial, physical evidence of the baptism with the Spirit. It should also be evident that there is little to warrant the exaggerated emphasis placed on glossolalia by many in our day.

There is a sense in which knowledge, prophecies, and languages were to cease (1 Cor. 13:8-10). Many understand this to mean that the completion of the New Testament meant no further need for these particular gifts.

It is, however, entirely possible that there may be genuine language gifts today as at other times in the history of the Church. All over the world, missionaries are telling the wonderful works of God in the languages of the people to whom they preach. They did not acquire these languages right out of the blue. But in hundreds of instances they have been able to communicate the gospel far sooner and more effectively than they ever could with unaided human skills or learning.

In fact, most of the gifts listed both in Romans and in 1 Corinthians are related to human abilities. They are subject to development and enlargement under the Spirit's power.

Rarely does speaking to men to edification, exhortation, and comfort ("the word of wisdom" and "the word of knowledge") come fully developed instantaneously. Serving, teaching, encouraging, giving, leadership—all involve skills that are acquired as well as powers divinely imparted.

Even instances of divine healing are often cases where the healing process is greatly shortened. They are not always instantaneous. It is with us as with the boy described in the Gospels—from that hour he began to get well. The crisis was past. Healing had begun.

God is the God of the supernatural. But He doesn't always come in the earthquake, the thunder, or the lightning. Often He comes in the "still small voice." It is no less important to recognize His coming in the "still small voice" than it is to see Him in the earthquake, the thunder, or the lightning.

# 6

# The Gifts and the Fruit

One additional point must be considered. Because the service gifts are so important in the life of the body (the church) and because they are given by the Spirit, there is a tendency to regard them as measures of spirituality.

The Apostle Paul distinguishes between "the natural man," the "carnal" man, and the "spiritual" man (1 Cor. 2:14—3:3, KJV). The natural man is void of real spiritual life—"the man without the Spirit" (1 Cor. 2:14). He is "dead in . . . transgressions and sins" (Eph. 2:1). The carnal are "babes in Christ" (KJV) whose personal and church life is marred by "jealousy and quarreling" (1 Cor. 3:3).

The spiritual man, on the other hand, represents Christianity at its New Testament norm. He understands and discerns the things of the Spirit. His life is lived, not by standards of human judgment alone, but according to the mind of Christ (1 Cor. 2:14-15). Such is the person who has claimed the promise of Jesus, "If you love me, you will do what I command. I will ask the Father, and he will give you another Counselor, the Spirit of truth, to be with you forever. The world cannot accept this Counselor, because it neither sees him nor knows him. But you know him, for he lives with you and will be in you" (John 14:15-17). This promise, as we have seen, is personal as well as dispensational. For when Jesus did ask the Father, He said, "My prayer is not for them alone. I pray also for those who will believe in me through their message" (John 17:20).

But what are the marks of the spiritual Christian? Is there a measure of spirituality in the New Testament? If so, is it to be found in one or even many of the service gifts?

The answers are: There are indeed marks and measures of the spiritual life in the New Testament. But the criteria of spirituality are not any one or more of the gifts of the Spirit. They are to be found in New Testament teachings as to what the Holy Spirit is like and in what the Apostle Paul called "the fruit of the Spirit."

## I. SPIRITLIKE

"Spiritual" in the New Testament is literally "Spiritlike" *(pneumatikos)*. It has to do with attitudes, dispositions, traits of character, and motivations that are conditioned by the indwelling Holy Spirit. The spiritual Christian is still thoroughly human. He makes no claim to perfection of personality or performance. His likeness to the Holy Spirit is far from complete. Rather it is growing and progressing. But the measure of the Spirit's infilling is a growing likeness to Him.

What is the Holy Spirit like? He is variously described in the Bible as the Spirit of Christ, of holiness, of compassion, of love, of soundness of mind (e.g., Rom. 1:4; 8:9; 2 Tim. 1:7, KJV). But the most expressive description of what the Holy Spirit is like is given in the promise of Jesus in John 14:16—the Father "will give you *another* Counselor."

The truth is much more emphatic in the Greek New Testament than it is in English. Greek has two main words for "other" or "another." One is *heteros.* This means "another of a different kind," as when we speak of false doctrine as "heterodoxy," "doctrine of another kind." The second word is *allos*. It means "another of the same kind." Jesus said, "I will ask the Father, and he will give you *[allos parakletos]*"—another Comforter, Helper, or Counselor, One of the same kind, One just like Me—literally, "another Jesus."

When we want to know what God is like, we look at Jesus. "Anyone who has seen me," Jesus said, "has seen the Father" (John 14:9). In just the same way, when we want to know what the Holy Spirit is like, we should also look at Jesus—"He will give you Another just like Me."

What this means is obvious. The spiritual Christian is the Christlike Christian. The first measure and mark of spirituality in the New Testament is Christlikeness. No person is genuinely spiritual who is markedly unlike Christ. Growing in spirituality is growing in Christlikeness. "More like the Master" means more deeply spiritual.

## II. THE FRUIT OF THE SPIRIT

The concept of Christlikeness itself gains new depth in a list of graces Paul called simply "the fruit of the Spirit." In a striking contrast between the works of the flesh and "the fruit of the Spirit," Paul writes, "But the fruit of the Spirit is love, joy, peace, patience, kindness, goodness, faithfulness, gentleness and self-control" (Gal. 5:22-23).

Jesus himself had underlined the importance of "fruit." He never suggested, "By their *gifts* you shall know them." He did distinguish the true from the false by twice remarking, "By their fruit you will recognize them" (Matt. 7:16, 20). Just as grapevines bear grapes, and fig trees bear figs, so good trees bear good fruit and "a bad tree bears bad fruit" (vv. 16-18).

Jesus never suggested that the Gardener Father "cuts off every branch" from the Vine that is not abundantly and obviously gifted. He did say, "I am the true vine and my

Father is the gardener. He cuts off every branch in me that bears no fruit, while every branch that does bear fruit he trims clean so that it will be even more fruitful. . . . If a man remains in me and I in him, he will bear much fruit; apart from me you can do nothing. If anyone does not remain in me, he is like a branch that is thrown away and withers; such branches are picked up, thrown into the fire and burned" (John 15:1-6).

Fruit, then, is the decisive indicator of the kind of inner life. "This is to my Father's glory, that you bear much fruit, showing yourselves to be my disciples" (John 15:8). The quality of fruit marks the quality of the life within and much fruit glorifies the Father.

But Paul's grammar in Gal. 5:22-23 is admittedly strange. "The fruit of the Spirit *is*," he said; and then goes on to list nine graces or qualities of character: "love, joy, peace, patience, kindness, goodness, faithfulness, gentleness, and self-control." The sentence form would seem to call for "The fruits of the Spirit *are* love, joy, peace, patience, kindness"—and so on.

There are two possible explanations of this manner of speaking.

## 1. An Indivisible Cluster

It is possible that the apostle means to say that the fruit of the Spirit is an indivisible cluster of graces that belong together and go together. They are not separable qualities or graces that may be divided up—that is, when they are present in life as the fruit of the Spirit.

Here is a conspicuous difference between the fruit of the Spirit and the gifts of the Spirit. As we have seen, Paul repeatedly insists that the gifts of the Spirit are given differently to different persons as different members of a physical body have different functions (1 Cor. 12:7-11, 14-

27, 29-30). The fruit of the Spirit is in complete contrast to this. One Christian does not have the grace of love, another joy, a third peace, a fourth patience, a fifth kindness, and so on—although differences of temperament and personality may tend to emphasize one or another of these graces. Rather, all together—"love, joy, peace, patience, kindness, goodness, faithfulness, gentleness, self-control"—are the unified and indivisible fruit of the Spirit.

## 2. A Description of Christlike Love

But there is another possible explanation of the grammar in Gal. 5:22-23. It lies in the thought that Paul means to say, "The fruit of the Spirit is LOVE—love that is joyous, serene, patient, kind, good, faithful, gentle, and self-controlled." S. D. Gordon once suggested that joy is love singing, peace is love resting, patience is love enduring, kindness is love sharing, goodness is love's character, faithfulness is love's habit, gentleness is love's touch, and self-control is love in charge.

It is to be noted that the context of each list of gifts is the expression of love. Peter says, "Above all, love each other deeply, because love covers over a multitude of sins. . . . Each one should use whatever spiritual gift he has received to serve others, faithfully administering God's grace in its various forms" (1 Pet. 4:8-10).

Paul immediately follows his list of service gifts in Romans 12 with the words, "Love must be sincere. . . . Be devoted to one another in brotherly love" (vv. 9-10). In the next chapter, he proclaims love as the fulfillment of the law. All commandments "are summed up in this one rule: 'Love your neighbor as yourself'" (13:8-10).

In his most misunderstood passage, the apostle most stresses the key importance of love. He closes his discussion of charismata in 1 Corinthians 12 with the words, "And now

I will show you the most excellent way" (v. 31). It is his prelude to the great "Hymn to Love" in 1 Corinthians 13. Even 1 Corinthians 14, with its unfavorable comparison between speaking unfamiliar languages and speaking to others "for their strengthening, encouragement and comfort" (v. 3), opens with the words, "Follow the way of love and eagerly desire spiritual gifts, especially the gift of prophecy" (v. 1).

Nothing can make up for lack of love. "If I speak in the tongues of men and of angels, but have not love, I am only a resounding gong or a clanging cymbal. If I have the gift of prophecy, and can fathom all mysteries and all knowledge, and if I have a faith that can move mountains, but have not love, I am nothing. If I give all I possess to the poor and surrender my body to the flames, but have not love, I gain nothing" (1 Cor. 13:1-3).

To use the presence or absence of gifts as a basis of judgment about another's spirituality is to abuse them and completely to misunderstand their purpose and meaning. Love is the fruit, and love is the measure, and any or all gifts together without love mean nothing as far as spirituality goes.

How can I measure the spiritual dimension of my life? It is to the extent that I manifest God's love—His joyous, serene, patient, kind, good, faithful, gentle, and self-controlled love.

"Love is patient, love is kind. It does not envy, it does not boast, it is not proud. It is not rude, it is not self-seeking, it is not easily angered, it keeps no record of wrongs. Love does not delight in evil but rejoices in the truth. It always protects, always trusts, always hopes, always perseveres.

"Love never fails. But where there are prophecies, they will cease; where there are tongues, they will be stilled;

where there is knowledge, it will pass away. For we know in part and we prophesy in part, but when perfection comes, the imperfect disappears. When I was a child, I talked like a child, I thought like a child, I reasoned like a child. When I became a man, I put childish ways behind me. Now we see but a poor reflection; then we shall see face to face. Now I know in part; then I shall know fully, even as I am fully known.

"And now these three remain: faith, hope and love. But the greatest of these is love" (1 Cor. 13:4-13).

# Reference Notes

PREFACE

1. Thomas a Kempis, *On the Imitation of Christ*, trans. Richard Whitford (Philadelphia: John C. Winston Co., n.d.), 3:vi:116.

CHAPTER 1. THE GIVER AS GIFT

1. Daniel Steele, *The Gospel of the Comforter* (Chicago: The Christian Witness Co., 1917), pp. 26-31.

2. The NIV completely misses the meaning of the original Greek in its translation of Acts 11:17. This verse literally reads, "having believed on the Lord Jesus," indicating that the disciples were believers when they received the promise of the Father. Also "saved" (Acts 15:11) in the NT includes more than initial conversion (cf. 2 Thess. 2:13).

CHAPTER 2. WHAT ARE SPIRITUAL GIFTS?

1. Archibald M. Hunter, *Probing the New Testament* (Richmond, Va.: John Knox Press, 1971), p. 89.

2. H. Orton Wiley, *Christian Theology* (Kansas City, Mo.: Beacon Hill Press, 1941), 2:317.

3. *Ibid.*, p. 318.

4. *Report of the Special Committee on the Work of the Holy Spirit.* To the 182nd General Assembly of the United Presbyterian Church in the United States of America (Philadelphia: Office of the General Assembly, 1970), p. 39.

5. Cf. Ray C. Stedman, *Body Life* (Glendale, Calif.: Regal Books, 1972).

CHAPTER 3. THE ROMANS LIST

1. Stephen F. Winward, *Teach Yourself to Pray* (New York: Harper and Brothers Publishers, 1961), p. 54.

2. Quoted by William Barclay in *Daily Celebration. Devotional Readings for Every Day of the Year* (Waco, Tex.: Word Books, Publisher, 1971), p. 236.

3. J. B. Chapman, *Herald of Holiness*, 15, no. 8 (May 19, 1926):2.

Chapter 4. The Corinthians List

1. Peter Forsyth, *The Cure of Souls: An Anthology of P. T. Forsyth's Practical Writings*, ed. Harry Escott (Grand Rapids, Mich.: William B. Eerdmans Publishing Co., 1971), p. 95.

2. Paul Tillich, *The Eternal Now* (New York: Charles Scribner's Sons, 1963), pp. 164-65.

3. Norman Snaith, *Hymns of the Temple* (London: SCM Press, Ltd., 1951), p. 82.

Chapter 5. The Language Gifts

1. Cf. William J. Samarin, *Tongues of Men and Angels. The Religious Language of Pentecostalism* (New York: The Macmillan Co., 1972), p. 65.

2. Vinson Synan, *The Holiness-Pentecostal Movement in the United States* (Grand Rapids, Mich.: William B. Eerdmans Publishing Co., 1971), p. 99, fn. 12.

3. Marvin R. Vincent, *Word Studies in the New Testament* (Grand Rapids, Mich.: William B. Eerdmans Co., 1946), p. 269.

4. Kenneth Wuest, *The New Testament: An Expanded Translation* (Grand Rapids, Mich.: William B. Eerdmans Publishing Co., 1961), *in loc.*

5. Cf. Harvey J. S. Blaney, *Speaking in Unknown Tongues: The Pauline Position* (Kansas City: Beacon Hill Press of Kansas City, 1973), pp. 20-21. See also the careful study by Dr. Charles D. Isbell, "Glossolalia and Propheteialalia: A Study of 1 Corinthians 14," *Wesleyan Theological Journal*, Vol. 10 (spring, 1975).